It's Easy To Play Ballads.

Wise Publications
London/New York/Sydney

Exclusive Distributors:
Music Sales Limited
8/9 Frith Street, London, W1V 5TZ, England.
Music Sales Pty. Limited
120 Rothschild Avenue, Rosebery, NSW 2018, Australia.

This book © Copyright 1986 by
Wise Publications
ISBN 0.7119.0918.0
Order No. AM 63025

Art Direction by Mike Bell
Cover illustration by Conny Jude
Arranged by Christopher Norton
Compiled by Peter Evans

Music Sales complete catalogue lists thousands
of titles and is free from your local music
book shop, or direct from Music Sales Limited.
Please send a cheque or Postal Order for £1·50 for postage to
Music Sales Limited, 8/9 Frith Street, London W1V 5TZ, England.

Printed in England by
Caligraving Limited
Thetford Norfolk

Love Is Blue
(L'Amour Est Bleu)

Music by Andre Popp
Original Words by Pierre Cour
English Lyric by Bryan Blackburn

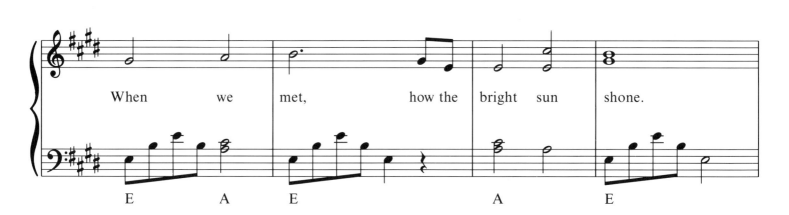

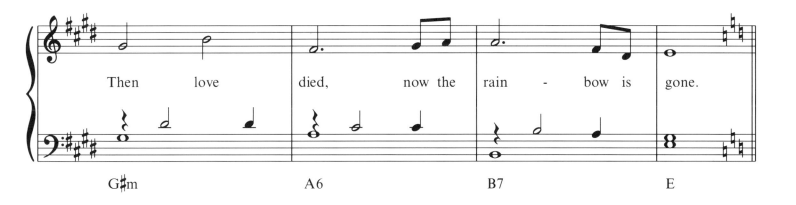

Then love died, now the rain - bow is gone.

G#m   A6   B7   E

Black, black, the nights I've known, long - ing for you, so

Em   A   D   G   Em   C

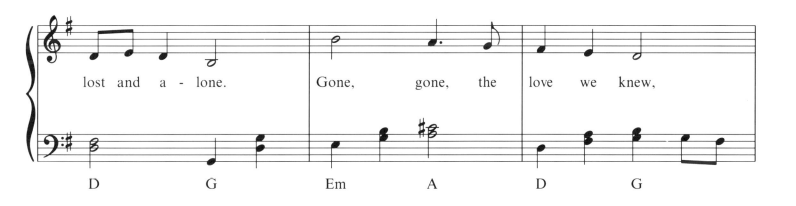

lost and a - lone. Gone, gone, the love we knew,

D   G   Em   A   D   G

1.
blue is my world, now | I'm with-out you. _____

2.
I'm with-out you.
rit.

Em   C   B7   Em   B7   Em

Nights In White Satin

Words & Music by Justin Hayward

That Ole Devil Called Love

Words & Music by Doris Fisher & Allan Roberts

Sometimes When We Touch

Words & Music by Dan Hill & Barry Mann

12

13

Fool
(If You Think It's Over)

Words & Music by Chris Rea

Moderato

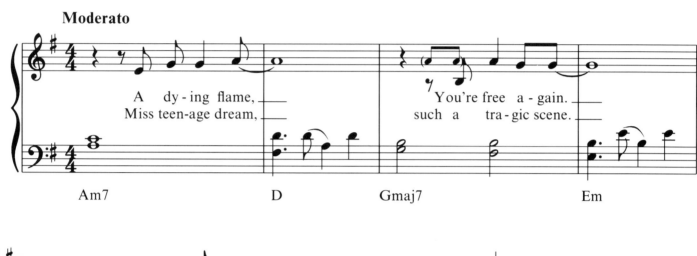

A dy-ing flame, _____ You're free a - gain. _____
Miss teen-age dream, _____ such a tra-gic scene. _____

Am7   D   Gmaj7   Em

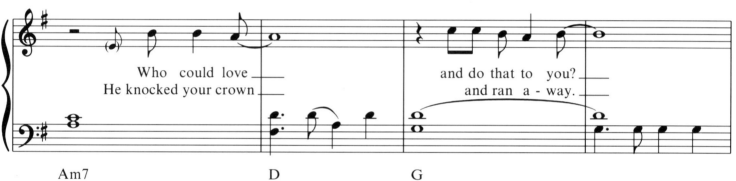

Who could love _____ and do that to you? _____
He knocked your crown _____ and ran a - way. _____

Am7   D   G

All dressed in black, _____ he won't be com - ing back.
First wound of pride, _____ but how you cried _____ and cried.

Am7   D   Gmaj7   Em

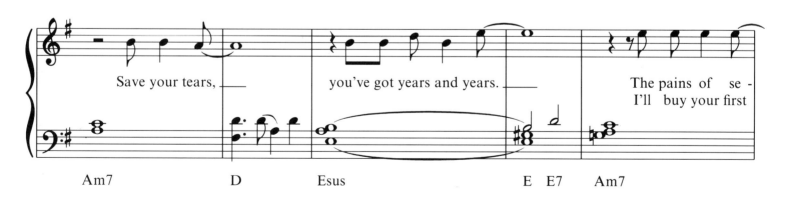

Save your tears, _____ you've got years and years. _____ The pains of se -
I'll buy your first

Am7   D   Esus   E   E7   Am7

Let Me Try Again

Music by Caravelli
French Words by Michel Jourdan
English Words by Paul Anka & Sammy Cahn

stay.
mask.

Dm7   G7   C   Am   Dm7   G7

CHORUS: Let me try   a - gain,   let me try   a -

gain.   Think of all   we   had be - fore,

Cmaj7   Bm7 ♭5   E ♯5   E   Am   Am/G

let me try   once   more. _____   We can have   it

C/D   D7   G7sus   G7   C   Am

all,   you and I   a - gain.

Dm7   G7   Cmaj7

Just for-give   me   or I'll die, please let me   try   a - gain.

Bm7 ♭5   E ♯5   E   Am   Dm   G7sus G7   C

This Guy's In Love With You

Words by Hal David
Music by Burt Bacharach

Moderately slow

You see ___ this guy, ___ this guy's in love with you.

Eb *Abmaj7*

Yes, I'm ___ in love. ___ Who looks at you the

This guy's in love, ___ and what I'd do to

Dbmaj7 *Eb* *Abmaj7* *Gsus* *G7*

way I do? ___ When you smile, ___ I can tell we

make you mine. ___ Tell me how, ___ is it so? Don't

Cm *Bbmin* *Eb9*

know each oth-er ve-ry well. How can I show you I'm

let me be the last to know. My hands are sha-king. Don't

Abmaj7 *Abm6* *Gm7* *Cm*

19

I'll Never Smile Again, (Until I Smile At You)

Words & Music by Ruth Lowe

Try A Little Tenderness

Words & Music by Harry Woods,
Jimmy Campbell & Reg Connelly

It's not just sen-ti-men-tal, she has her grief and

C7   F   E7   Am

care,   and a   word _____ that's soft and   gen - tle,   makes it

A7   Dm   A7

ea - si - er   to   bear.   You won't re - gret it,

Dm   Gsus   G   C

wo-man don't for-get it,   love is their whole hap - pi - ness.   It's all so ea-sy,

Dm7   G7   C   Gm/B♭   A   D7

| 1 | | | 2   **D.C.** |

try a lit-tle ten - der - ness.   — ness.

F6   Dm7   G7   C   G7   C

Annie's Song

Words & Music by John Denver

Moderato

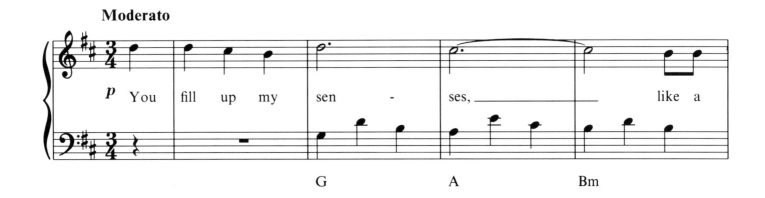

You fill up my sen - ses, _____ like a

G   A   Bm

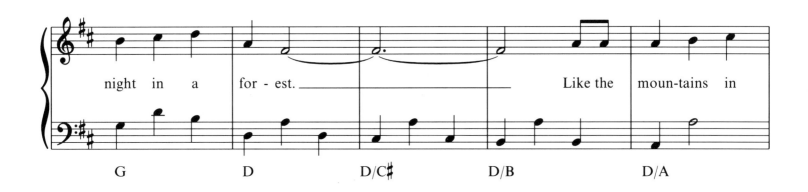

night in a for - est. _____ Like the moun-tains in

G   D   D/C♯   D/B   D/A

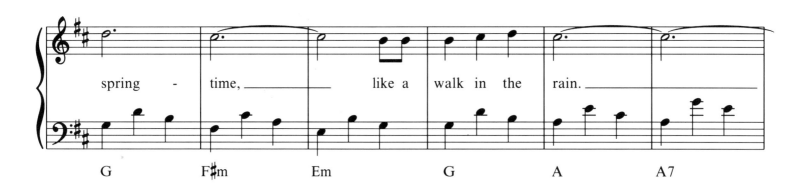

spring - time, _____ like a walk in the rain. _____

G   F♯m   Em   G   A   A7

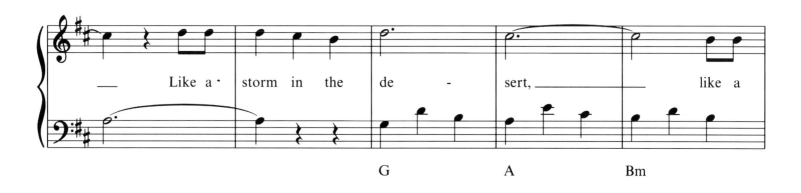

Like a storm in the de - sert, _____ like a

G   A   Bm

arms. _____ Let me lay down be - side
rain. _____ Like a storm in the de -

A   A7   G

you, _____ let me al - ways be with you. _____
sert, _____ like a sleep - y blue o - cean. _____

A   Bm   G   D   D/C♯

___   You   Come let me love   you, _____   come
___   You   fill up my ses - ses, _____   come

D/B   D/A   G   F♯m   Em

1.

love me a - gain. _____   You fill up my
fill me a -

A   D   Dsus   D   Dsus

2

- gain. _____   *rit.*

D   Dsus   D   Dsus   D   Dsus   D

Feelings
(Dime)

English Words & Music by Morris Albert
Spanish Lyric by Thomas Fundora

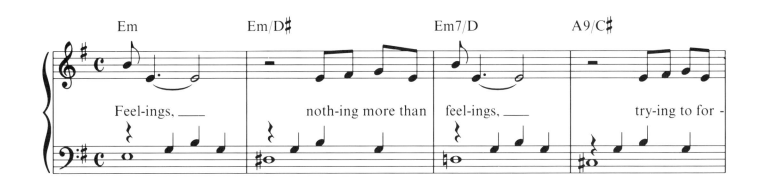

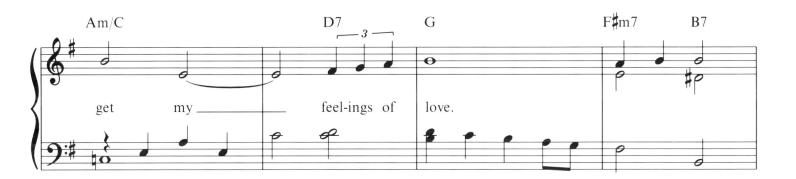

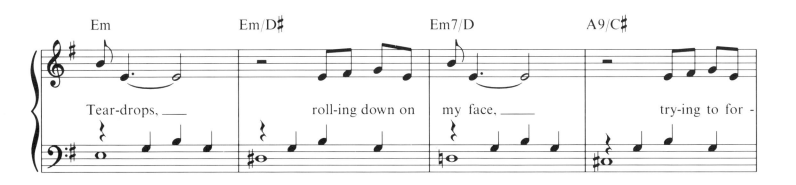

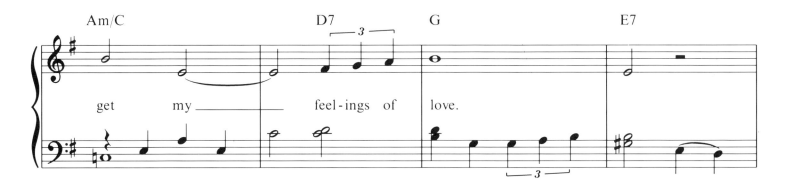

Feel -ings, _____ _____ for all my life I'll feel it, I wish I'd nev-er

met you, girl, you'll nev-er come a - gain. _____

Feel - ings, wo wo wo feel - ings, wo wo wo

feel you a - gain in my arms.

Feel-ings, _____ feel-ings like I've nev - er lost you _____ and feel-ings like I'll

nev - er have you___ a-gain in my heart.

As Time Goes By

Words & Music by Herman Hupfeld

Moderato

E°   F7   D°   B♭m/D♭   B♭°/D♭   C7♯5   C7

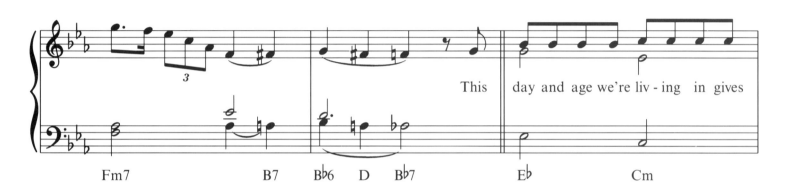

This day and age we're liv-ing in gives

Fm7   B7   B♭6   D   B♭7   E♭   Cm

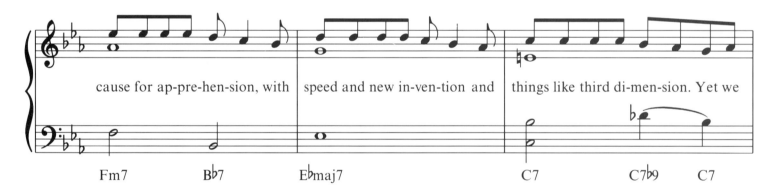

cause for ap-pre-hen-sion, with speed and new in-ven-tion and things like third di-men-sion. Yet we

Fm7   B♭7   E♭maj7   C7   C7♭9   C7

get a tri-fle wea-ry with Mis-ter Ein-stein's theo-ry, so we must get down to earth at times, re-

Fm   B♭7   E♭   G7   Cm   B♭   D7

brings, as time goes by. _____ Moon-light and love - songs

Fm7 Bb7 Fm7 Bb7   Eb   Ab   G7   Eb Eb7   Ab

ne - ver out of date, hearts full of pas - sion, jea - lou-sy and hate.

C7   Fm7   F#o

Wo-man needs man and man must have his mate, that no - one can de - ny. _____ It's

Cm   F#o   F7   Bb9   Eo   Bb7

still the same old sto-ry, a fight for love and glo-ry, a case of do or die! _____ The

Fm   Bb7   Gm7b5   Bb7   Eb Ebm6 Eb6   Cm   Gm

1.
world will al-ways wel-come lo - vers, as time goes by. You

2.
by.

F7   Gm7 Eb Gm Eo   Fm7 Bb7   Eb   Eb

Against All Odds
(Take A Look At Me Now)

Words & Music by Phil Collins

2. How can you just walk away from me,
When all I can do is watch you leave?
'Cause we shared the laughter and the pain,
And even shared the tears.
You're the only one who really knew me at all.
Chorus:

3. I wish I could just make you turn around,
Turn around and see me cry.
There's so much I need to say to you,
So many reasons why.
You're the only one who really knew me at all.
Chorus:

Morning Of My Life
(In The Morning)

Words & Music by Barry Alan Gibb

The Power Of Love

Words & Music by C. deRouge, G. Mende,
J. Rush & S. Applegate

Bb/D
F

I could ____ not for - sake _____ 'Cause I am your la -
al - ways ____ by your side. _____

Bb
Eb
Eb/D

- dy _____ and you are my man _____ when-ev-er you reach

Cm
F

____ for me _____ I'll do all that I can _____

1.
I'll do all that I can ____

____ Ev-en tho' there may be
2.
we're head-ing for
Bb
some - thing, _____

Eb
Eb/D

some-where I've nev-er been, _____ some-times I am fright-

43

Separate Lives

Words & Music by Stephen Bishop

feel lone-ly too?   You have no

right_____ to ask me how I feel.   You have no

right   to speak to me so kind._____ I can't go on,   hold-ing on to

ties,   now that we're liv-ing   sep-'rate lives.

2. Well I held   lives.   It's so ty-pi-cal,__ love

leads to i-so-la-tion. So you build that wall, so you

D.S. al Coda

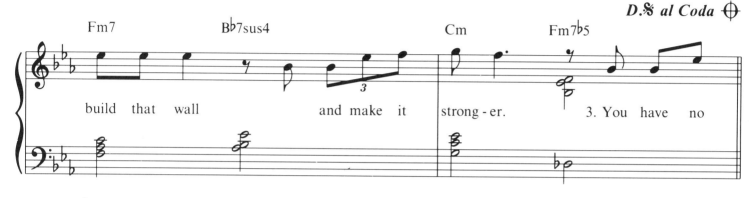

build that wall and make it strong-er. 3. You have no

CODA

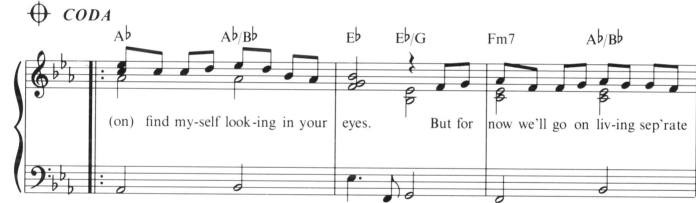

(on) find my-self look-ing in your eyes. But for now we'll go on liv-ing sep'rate

lives, Yes for now we'll go on liv-ing sep-'rate lives.

Chorus 2:   Well, I held on to let you go.
And if you lost your love for me,
you never let it show.
There was no way to compromise.
So now we're living separate lives.

Chorus 3:   You have no right to ask me how I feel.
You have no right to speak to me so kind.
Someday I might find myself looking in your eyes.
But for now, we'll go on living separate lives.
Yes, for now we'll go on living separate lives.

11/01 (41948)